Helen, Ethel & The Crazy Quilt

Based on the 1890 Letters
Between Helen Keller and Ethel Orr

Nancy Orr Johnson Jensen
Illustrated by Dawn Peterson

Mayhaven Publishing
P O Box 557
Mahomet, IL 61853
USA

Illustrations: Copyright © Dawn Peterson
Copyright © Nancy Orr Johnson Jensen
First Edition—First Printing 2007
1 2 3 4 5 6 7 8 9 10
Library of Congress Control Number: 2006939989
ISBN-10: 193227810-9
ISBN-13: 978-193227810-1

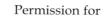

Permission for
Ms. Keller's quotes are courtesy of the AFB Press,
American Foundation for the Blind

Helen Keller Photo used by permission
Perkins School for the Blind, Watertown, MA

The quilt blocks and basket were photographed by
Kirsten Jensen Vondrak

Printed in Canada

This book is dedicated to all the descendants of
Ethel Orr and to those who have found inspiration in
Helen Keller's life.

Helen Keller at about the age when she and
Ethel Orr corresponded.

Photo used by permission Perkins School for the Blind, Watertown, MA

Ethel Orr outside her Bailey Island home. Her mother, who designed and created the quilt, and probably helped Ethel write her letters to Helen, can be seen sitting on the steps in the background. The woman on the right is unknown.

Pictured above is Mary Louise Orr, Ethel's mother. It was the beautiful quilt she was making during the winters of 1889 and 1890 that inspired her daughter Ethel to write to Helen Keller.

About this Book

In the winter of 1890, ten-year-old Ethel Orr, with a little help from her mother, wrote a letter to the famous ten-year-old Helen Keller. Ethel's letters have never been found, but Helen's responses to them were kept in the Orr family. This story is based on those letters and other artifacts. Two of these letters have never before been published.

"We are never really happy until we try
to brighten the lives of others."

—Helen Keller

The Crazy Quilt

The wind howled around the corners of the house and the sleet pounded against the windowpanes. 1890 was a rough winter along the coast of Maine.

Ten-year-old Ethel Orr was snug in her two-story frame house. Because she had asthma, she didn't attend school. Instead, she stayed home with her mother, Mary Louise Orr, on little Bailey Island. Her father, Captain James Orr, was far away, a mate on a sailing ship traveling around the world.

As Ethel practiced her piano on that blustery January day, her mother sat stitching the last section of the Crazy Quilt she had been working on for nearly a year. Here and there on the squares of the quilt were white silk ribbons with signatures from some very famous people.

Mrs. Orr stopped to examine her work. "This would be an excellent spot for one last signature," she said. "And I have an idea of the perfect famous person to ask."

She put down her quilt and walked to the credenza. "I read all about her, Ethel."

Ethel paused, her fingers suspended over the keys, then commenced practicing as her mother searched for the article.

"Here it is!" Mrs. Orr exclaimed. She carried the magazine back to her chair. "She is from Alabama. Her name is Helen Keller and there is even a picture of her. My goodness, she is ten years old—the same as you, Ethel! It says she was only a baby, 19-months-old, when she became very sick with a high fever. The illness left her deaf, blind, and mute."

Ethel stopped playing and went to look at the picture. "Is that why she's famous?"

"Oh, no. She's famous because she has learned to read and write so quickly, even though she can't see or hear. Her teacher, Annie Sullivan, took Helen to the Perkins Institution for the Blind in Boston just two years ago to learn with other blind boys and girls."

"She is lucky to go to school with other children," Ethel murmured. "I wish I could."

Her mother looked sweetly at her. "You will someday, when your asthma is not so bothersome."

Ethel continued to look at the photograph.

"I want to write to this Helen right now," she said. "I will send a silk ribbon and if she signs it maybe your quilt will also be famous one day."

Ethel's mother smiled, put the magazine aside and continued stitching on her beautiful quilt.

Ethel sat down at a little desk by the window overlooking the bay and took out some writing paper and a pencil. First she closed her eyes, pretending to be blind. Then she wrote, "Dear Helen, My name is Ethel Orr and I am ten years old." When she opened her eyes she looked at what she had written. She could hardly read anything. The words all ran

together, first uphill and then down.

"Mother, I can't believe Helen Keller can write so that anyone can understand her words."

Ethel's mother looked up. "It says in the article that Miss Sullivan taught Helen to use Square Handwriting. She uses a grooved board with a paper resting over it. She writes within the grooves, which guide her pencil. That helps her write in a straight line. I would guess she puts a finger or spacer of some type between the letters so they don't all run together."

Ethel frowned. "But how did Helen learn how to write if she can't hear or see?"

"According to the article, Miss Sullivan spells out words with her fingers in Helen's hands. It is called, let's see…oh yes, the Manual Alphabet. She started using this method of teaching the very first day she worked with Helen. After repeatedly spelling words in Helen's hand, and having her touch an object the word represented, Helen began to realize that everything has a name."

Ethel started again to write her letter to Helen, her eyes wide open. Frequently, though, her mother helped her with spelling and how to express herself.

Bailey Island, Maine

January 25, 1890

Dear Helen,

My name is Ethel Orr and I am ten years old, the same age as you. I live on an island off the coast of Maine. I do not attend school because I have asthma so my mother teaches me at home.

I have one pet. It is a parrot. I am teaching her to talk. Do you have any pets?

My mother is making a Crazy Quilt and I would like you to sign the silk ribbon that I put in the envelope. When it comes back to me, Mother will sew it on one of the quilt squares with some pretty velvet flowers around it.

Mother has almost completed putting the quilt together after working on it for nearly a year. She painted animals found on the island and beautiful ladies' faces on some squares. She also made fans of silk with fancy stitches all around them. Some famous people have signed silk ribbons for it: The first lady of the United States, Carolyn Harrison; the Vice President's wife, Anna Morton; and John Greenleaf Whittier, the famous poet. I hope you will sign the silk ribbon for Mother's quilt because I think you are famous, too.

Your friend,
Ethel

> "The best and most beautiful things in the world
> cannot be seen or even touched,
> but just felt in the heart."
>
> —Helen Keller

The First Letter

Ethel's mother put the letter and a little silk ribbon into an envelope and addressed it to Tuscumbia, Alabama, the address noted in the magazine.

"Do you think we will hear back soon, Mother?" Ethel asked as she fed bits of cracker to Polly, the colorful parrot her father had brought home from one of his long trips to the South Seas.

"I don't know, Ethel. We can only wait patiently."

Weeks went by without a reply. Every afternoon Ethel watched the bay from the front window as the steamboat bearing the mail and supplies for Bailey Island slowly chugged into Lowell's Cove. She watched as Mr. York, the postmaster, waited at the wharf for the mail and supplies to be loaded onto his wagon. She watched as his horse pulled the wagon over the rutted dirt road to the building atop the neighboring hill. It housed both the post office and the general store.

As Ethel sat day-dreaming, her mother walked into the room. "Ethel, you have been inside this house for too long and this is a beautiful spring day. Let's get bundled up and go to the post office. Who knows, perhaps we will hear from Helen today."

Ethel hurried up the stairs to her room and readied herself. She put on her lightweight coat her mother had made using wool from Scotland, her favorite scarf and mittens knitted by her Aunt Lizzie, and a knit cap her grandmother had given her that slid all the way down over her ears. When she got to the front door she pulled on her heavy boots, knowing the mud would be deep from the melting snow.

When they arrived at the post office the usual crowd of islanders was there, chatting about the unexpected thaw as they waited for the mail to be sorted.

At last, the little grated window opened and the postmaster announced that the mail was ready. Ethel and her mother waited their turn.

"Mrs. Orr, it seems you have little mail today, except a letter to Ethel all the way from Boston, Massachusetts. Ethel looked at her mother. "From Boston?" Could this be the letter from Helen Keller?

Ethel took off her mittens, carefully opened the envelope, and slid out a letter. On it were neat block letters. Ethel looked again into the envelope and turned to her mother. "There is no ribbon." She could hardly keep the tears from flowing.

Her mother was also disappointed but she hid her feelings from Ethel.

"Read the letter, dear, and see what Helen has to say."

South Boston   February 26, 1890

Dear Little Friend Ethel,

My dear mamma has just sent me your letter. I am very sorry that I cannot write my name on the ribbon for your quilt, because I am afraid you will be disappointed. I cannot use a pen and ink, because I am blind and pencil writing would soon rub out. I hope you will not feel very sad about it. It makes me very happy [to] know that you think of me for I love all little girls and boys very dearly. I am very far away from darling little sister, and my beautiful home. I am studying in Boston with my teacher. I would like so much to see your parrot. I have read about them, but have never yet seen one. What do you call him I am very fond [of] pets. I have a tiny canary and a pair [of] pigeons and a great mastiff, a kind gentleman is going to give me a gentle donkey when I go home. I hope you will soon be quite well and strong. I am sure you will enjoy going to school. It is beautiful [to] learn all about the strange and wonderful things in our world. I am studying the grasshopper now. Give my love [to] your mother and teach your parrot to say Helen.

Your loving little friend, H. A. Keller

After reading the letter, Ethel felt better. She was happy to find a new friend.

"Mother, when I get home, I'm going to fill a little box of treasures from far-away places that Grandfather and Father brought home from their journeys at sea. Then I'll send them to Helen."

"What a good idea, Ethel. We'll look through the old trunk and see what we have saved. Maybe we..."

Ethel interrupted, "Do you think I can teach Polly to say *Helen*?"

Her mother was pleased that Ethel showed such enthusiasm. "I'm sure you can."

Before they left the post office, Ethel thanked Mr. York for bringing the welcomed mail to them.

"It is always a pleasure, Miss Orr. Always a pleasure."

"Keep your face to the sunshine
and you cannot see the shadows."

—Helen Keller

Treasures

When they arrived home, Ethel placed Helen's cherished letter on her desk and went to Polly's cage. "Polly, say Helen. Helen. Hel-en." Ethel repeated slowly. "Hel-en. Hel-en."

The parrot made little squawks, but nothing sounded like Helen at all.

Ethel ran to the kitchen and returned with a stale piece of bread. She pinched off a piece and held it out to the bird. It plucked the little morsel from Ethel's outstretched hand and squawked a thank you.

"Polly, please say Helen. Hel-en."

Still, Polly only squawked.

Finally, Ethel gave up and joined her mother who was searching through the trunk for something special to send to Helen. Ethel knelt beside her.

Her mother pulled out a folding fan made of bamboo and silk. "You could send this to Helen. And look at this scroll with Chinese calligraphy. And here. How about sending her a hand-carved bookmark?"

It was nearly dark when they closed the lid on the trunk. Ethel followed her mother to the parlor to wrap the gifts in a small box. As Ethel walked by Polly she whispered, "Hel-en. Hel-en. Hel-en."

The parrot cocked her head to one side and looked at Ethel, then opened her beak and said the only word she had ever learned, "Hel-lo. Hel-lo."

The next day, after lunch, Ethel and her mother sat down to write to Helen. When they saw the boat chug into Lowell's Cove, they rushed to seal the letter, grabbed the little box of treasures and pulled on their wraps to walk to the post office.

As the days passed, the weather warmed. The ice and snow that had covered the shoreline melted entirely. One morning when the tide was low, Mrs. Orr said Ethel could go down to the shoreline and look for shells.

Ethel put on warm clothes and pulled on rubber boots that nearly reached her knees to keep her feet dry.

She stopped by the shed to get a small pail. As she walked down the path and onto the ledges, she was careful not to slip on the seaweed. After picking up several small periwinkles from the tidal pools, she headed to the water's edge. There she found sea urchins, star fish, limpet shells, and some sea glass. Her pail was filled to the brim.

When Ethel got to the house with her pail of sea treasures, her mother stopped her. "Ethel, leave the the pail outside. You can take the shells out and put them on the stoop to dry. Later we'll boil them in water to clean them."

"The most beautiful world is always
entered through imagination."

—Helen Keller

The Gift

One windy afternoon in March, Ethel's mother went to the post office. When she returned, she carried a little package for Ethel. It was postmarked Tuscumbia, Alabama. When Ethel opened it, she saw a small blue and white beaded basket with fluted edges and a little handle.

"Mother, look how beautiful this is. It's made of tiny glass beads. Do you think Helen made this?"

A few days later, a letter arrived from Boston.

Nancy Orr Johnson Jensen

So. Boston, March 15, 1890.
My Sweet Little Friend,

The box of pretty things you sent me, and your dear mother's letter have been received, and I do not know how to tell you how happy they made me. I love dearly to see things that have come from far away lands. Geography is a beautiful study. you will enjoy it I am sure, when you are well enough to go to school. A long while ago when I was a small child I did not know anything about the beautiful world, and all the strange and wonderful things that I know about now. I was not perfectly happy then. You must ask your kind mamma to tell me about Bailey's Island when she writes to me again. I hope Polly has learned to say Helen by this time. All of my friends were greatly interested in my pretty treasures. I am very glad that my mother sent you a little bead basket. Now I must tell my dear little Ethel good-bye for I have several letters to write before dinner.

With much love and a kiss from your little friend,
Helen A. Keller

Ethel wanted to send something else to her new friend. One day she picked through her shells, turning them over and over in her hand. She knew what she would do. She would send some of her favorite shells to Helen. She had cleaned and dried them. They would be a perfect gift from Bailey Island.

"Never bend your head.
Always hold it high.
Look the world straight in the face."
—Helen Keller

The Surprise

It was April and the smells and sounds of Spring filled the air. The red-winged blackbirds returned to the swamp by the cove. Wild roses along the path to the shore began to bud. Fishermen spread their nets in the fields to mend for another season. Lobstermen busied themselves making new traps.

Ethel's mother had finished her quilt and had proudly draped it over the quilt rack in the parlor. That afternoon she and Ethel walked to the post office. Everyone there chattered to one another as they were happy to see that Spring had finally arrived. As soon as the postmaster saw Ethel and her

mother he called, "I think I have something a little special for you. Here." He handed Ethel a letter. "Another letter from Boston. Who is writing you all the way from Boston, Ethel?"

Ethel turned the letter over in her hand. "Helen Keller. She's my friend."

Ethel opened the letter and unfolded the paper. Some flowers and butterfly cut-outs were pasted on the front.

So. Boston, Mass.
April 21st

My dear good little Ethel,

The box of shells and your dear mother's letter were received ever so long ago, and you must excuse me for not writing before. You are very kind to me and it makes me happy to have you love me. Very soon I shall learn about the little coral animal and the sponge, but now we are learning about the oyster and the clam. The other day I had a pretty cocoon given to me, and last Thursday a beautiful moth came out and laid some tiny eggs on my hand. I wish I had time to write you many interesting things but I have to study all day.

Lovingly yours, Helen

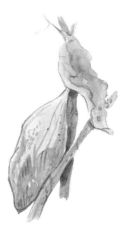

Ethel tucked the letter in her pocket and kept her hand on it all the way down the hill and through the field to their home by the cove.

Inside the house, Ethel took off her jacket and hung it on the hall tree. She went to the pantry, took a cookie from a jar on the shelf and walked over to Polly's cage. She broke the cookie into small chunks and kept them in her hand.

"Polly. Say Hel-en."

"Hello," said Polly.

Ethel put her face close to the cage, puckered her lips and whispered, "Hel-en." She held a piece of cookie even closer to Polly.

Polly dipped her head as if to play shy. She fluffed her feathers, and stretched her neck toward the sweet-smelling treat. She strutted around the cage.

Ethel withdrew the cookie and hid it behind her back. Polly craned her neck and peered here and there, looking for the treat. Finally, she looked at Ethel and clearly said, "Hel-en."

That night Ethel retrieved the letter and read it over and over. She tucked it beneath her pillow and fell asleep with a smile on her face. She was happy to have a new friend and was happy Polly had learned her friend's name.

Ethel didn't dream, but if she had, she might have dreamed about her mother's Crazy Quilt because long after Ethel would grow up, and long after her children, and her children's children were grown, her mother's quilt *would* become famous.

She didn't dream the quilt would be displayed on Bailey Island and in mainland towns nearby. Ethel didn't dream the quilt would be considered a masterpiece, that it would never show wear—though, by then, it would be well over 100 years old.

Ethel didn't dream that on a chilly day in March 2000 her descendants would take the quilt to the State of Maine Museum where it would be preserved. And when it was displayed, it would have the letters to Ethel from the world-famous Helen Keller displayed with it.

If Ethel had dreamed it, she would have smiled even more and dreamed the sweetest dreams.

Author's Note

At the time Helen Keller and my grandmother were corresponding, Helen was also writing to Alexander Graham Bell, John Greenleaf Whittier, Oliver Wendell Holmes, and Mark Twain.

At age ten Helen was also learning French, German and Latin.

In 1904, Helen graduated with honors from Radcliffe College in Cambridge, Massachusetts, called the "Harvard Annex" for women. She was the first deaf, blind, and mute person to have graduated from college.

It is interesting to note that while Helen Keller visited Alexander Graham Bell at his home in Nova Scotia, Mr. Bell was experimenting with kites by flying them tied to a wire instead of string. Helen mentioned to him that the wire could break. Helen had experienced stringing glass beads on wire and knew that wire *does* sometimes break. It is possible that she learned this while making bead baskets.

More About Square Handwriting

Square Handwriting was developed for the blind, probably in the early 1800's, at the Perkins Institution for the Blind in Boston, Massachusetts. Though there were other methods—Braille, for instance—Square Handwriting was the method Helen Keller used in writing to Ethel Orr.

This type of writing required paper, pencil and a grooved board of either cardboard or metal. The directions to write in this manner are very simple. The letters are simple and box-like with no complicated flourishes. Spacing is the hardest point to achieve.

If the writer is right handed, the left hand is used as a guide to feel where to place the pencil. If the writer is left handed, the right hand is used to feel for the groove.

Helen Keller, with Anne Sullivan's help, graduated from college, published her writing and spoke before many, many audiences over the course of her life. It may be that she remembered the letters from Ethel and the treasures she received from Bailey Island.

Bibliography

Garrett, Leslie. *Helen Keller*. New York: DK Publishing, Inc. 2004.

Keller, Helen. *The Story of My Life*. New York: Airmont Pub. Co., Inc., 1965.

Keller, Helen. *To Love This Life: Quotations*. New York: AFB Press, 2000.

Lash, Joseph P. *Helen and Teacher: The Story of Helen Keller and Anne Sullivan Macy*. New York: Dell Publishing Co., 1980.

Lawlor, Laurie. *Helen Keller: Rebellious Spirit*. New York: Holiday House, 2001.

Mellor, C. Michael. *Louis Braille — A Touch of Genius*. National Braille Press, Boston, 2006.

St. George, Judith. *Dear Dr. Bell. . . Your friend, Helen Keller*. New York: G. P. Putnam's Sons, 1992.

Schichtman, Sandra. *Helen Keller: Out of a Dark and Silent World*. Brookfield, Connecticut: The Millbrook Press, 2002.

Sutcliffe, Jane. *Helen Keller*. Minneapolis, Minnesota: Carolrhoda Books, Inc., 2002.

Keller, Helen; Sullivan, Annie; Macy, John Albert. *The Story of My Life; with her letters (1887-1901) and a supplementary account of her education, including passages from the reports and letters of her teacher, Anne Mansfield Sullivan by John Albert Macy.*

The Artifacts

Helen Keller's letters to Ethel, and her mother's quilt, are now housed at the State of Maine Museum in Augusta, Maine. The beaded basket is in a private collection.

On the following pages are photos of the actual artifacts: the letters, detail from the quilt, and the beaded basket. The lady in the veil is thought to be a self-portrait of Ethel's mother, Mary Louise Orr.

South Boston, Feb. 26, 1890.

Dear Little Friend Ethel,

My dear mamma has just sent me your letter. I am very sorry that I cannot write my name on the ribbon for your quilt, because I am afraid you will be disappointed. I cannot use a pen and ink, because I am blind and pencil writing would soon rub out. I hope you will not feel very sad about it. It makes me very happy know that you think of me for I love all little girls and boys very dearly. I am very far away from darling little sister, and my beautiful

home. I am studying in Boston
with my teacher. I would like
so much to see your parrot. I have
read about them, but have never
yet seen one. What do you call him
I am very fond pets. I have a tiny
canary and a pair pigeons and a
great mastiff, a kind gentleman
is going to give me a gentle donkey
when I go home. I hope you will
soon be quite well and strong.
I am sure you will enjoy going
to school. It is beautiful learn
all about the strange and wonderful things in our world. I am
studying the grasshopper now,
Give my love your mother and
teach your parrot to say Helen.
   Your loving little friend H. A. Keller.

So. Boston, March 15, 1890.

My sweet Little Friend,

The box of pretty things you sent me, and your dear mother's Letter have been received, and I do not know how to tell you how happy they made me. I love dearly to see things that have come from far away lands. Geography is a beautiful study—you will enjoy it I am sure, when you are well enough to go to school. A long while ago, when I was a small child I did not know anything about the beautiful world, and all the strange and wonderful things that I know about now. I was not perfectly happy then. You must ask your kind mamma to tell me about Baileys Island when she writes to me again. I hope Polly has learned to say Helen by this time. All of my friends were greatly interested in my pretty treasures. I am very glad that my mother sent you a little bead basket. Now I must tell my dear little Ethel good-bye, for I have several letters to write before dinner.

With much love and a kiss,
From your little friend,
Helen A. Keller.

So. Boston, Mass.,
April 21st

My dear good little Ethel,
The box of shells and
your dear mother's Let-
ter were received ever
so long ago, and you
must excuse me for not
writing before. You are
very kind to me, and it
makes me happy to have
you love me. Very soon,
I shall learn about

the little coral animal
and the sponge, but
now we are learning
about the oyster and the
clam. The other I had
a pretty cocoon given to
me, and last Thursday a
beautiful moth came
out, and laid some tiny
eggs on my hand. I wish
I had time to write you
many interesting things
but I have to study all day
Lovingly yours, Helen.

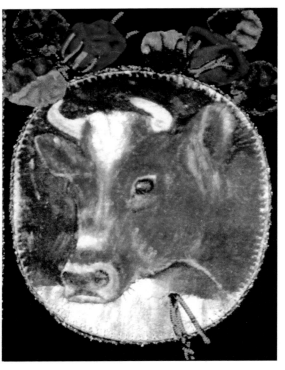

This basket was sent to Ethel
Orr in the spring of 1890. As
Helen was in Boston at this
time, it was sent by
her mother, Mrs. Keller.

—In private collection